SIGHT READING SUCCESS

PIANO GRADE 3

MALCOLM RILEY & PAUL TERRY

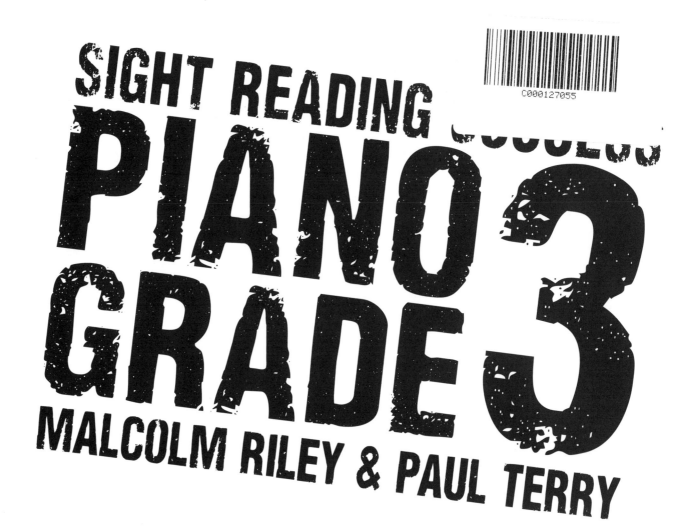

RHINEGOLD EDUCATION

WWW.RHINEGOLDEDUCATION.CO.UK

FOR STUDENTS

Sight reading is an important and enjoyable musical skill. The more you practise the better you will get, and working carefully through this book will help you.

Use the CD included with this book to hear how the pieces should sound. Listen to the music carefully to check your playing. Most of the written instructions are also spoken for you on the CD. The tracks can be downloaded onto an MP3 player if you find that easier to use next to the piano.

From the beginning of the book to piece 20 you should listen to the recording of each piece first to hear how it should sound (except when you are asked to do otherwise). Then play the music on the piano, copying what you have heard. From piece 21 onwards, make sure that you play first and then listen to check that you were correct. Up to piece 55 there are spoken reminders about important things to notice in the music, but after that you are on your own!

Tick the box when you have finished each section or piece, so that you know which ones you have tried – it's not sight reading if you keep playing the same pieces!

If you find any of the examples on the CD are too fast when you are starting out, there are software programs available on the internet that can slow down the speed of music on any CD played on a computer. One that is free to download is: **Speedshifter** (available from www.abrsm.org/en/students/speedshifter).

FOR TEACHERS

This book follows the sight reading requirements for the Grade 3 piano exam of the Associated Board of the Royal Schools of Music (as revised in 2009). It is also suitable for all piano students who wish to improve their sight reading skills.

A unique feature of the books in this series is the inclusion of a specially-recorded CD which students can use at home for additional guidance, and to check the accuracy of their own playing. Encourage your students to use it as a tool to evaluate their own playing and learn from their mistakes, as well as a support for when you are not there to help.

Sight Reading Success progressively introduces each of the elements in sight reading, along with many useful tips and exercises to improve fluency. Each book builds on the skills taught in the previous volumes, so it is recommended that your students work through Grades 1 and 2 before starting on this book.

The second part of the book includes exam-standard pieces to play in lessons or at home. Take a few minutes in every lesson to check progress and help with any difficulties, and encourage regular sight reading so that students have confidence when going into their exam.

Tick boxes are provided for students to record their progress through the book.

USING A METRONOME

A **metronome** is a device that will click a regular pulse at any speed you wish to help you keep in time when practising. There are several on the internet and the one at www.metronomeonline.com is free and easy to use. The numbers around the dial indicate the speed in beats (or pulses) per minute: the higher the number, the faster the speed.

RHYTHM AND TEMPO

 1 There are two new note lengths to learn for Grade 3 sight reading.

- The first is the **semiquaver** (or 16th note) ♪ .
  'Semi' means half, so a semiquaver is half the length of a quaver.

- Four semiquavers look like this and take the same amount of time as one crotchet.

- Two semiquavers take the same amount of time as one quaver.

Notice how semiquavers are joined by *two* beams (the lines joining the note stems).

A pair of semiquavers can be joined to a quaver (like this or this) if all of the notes fall within the same beat. This makes it easier to see where each beat starts when there are short notes in the music.

 2 Here is a clapping game that includes semiquavers. Listen to track 2 where you will hear that each one-bar pattern is followed by a gap for you to clap the pattern you have just heard. Keep to the pulse on the recording as you clap all four of these patterns.

 3 If you see semiquavers in a piece of sight reading, choose a pulse at which you can play these short notes really evenly, otherwise you may find it difficult to keep a steady beat throughout the music.

Here are three pieces with semiquaver patterns for you to sight read. For each piece, first clap the rhythm of the music, then listen to the recording and finally play it on the piano.

💿 **4** A dotted minim lasts for the same length of time as twelve semiquavers, so bars 2 and 4 in the next piece need very careful counting!

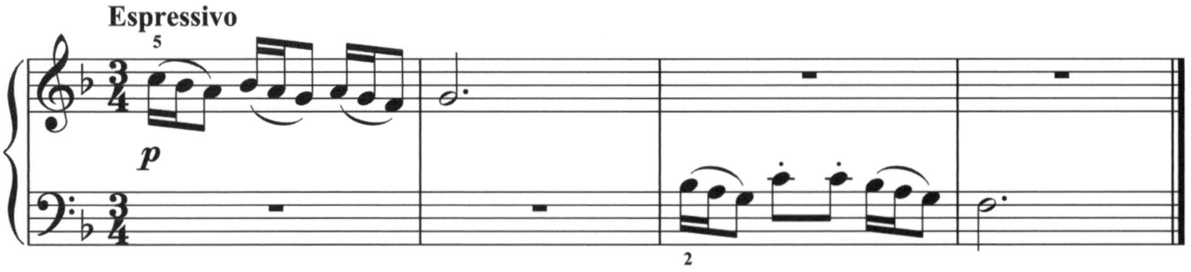

Pulse: ■ *1* ■ 2 ■ 3 ■ *1* ■ 2 ■ 3 ■ *1* ■ 2 ■ 3 ■ *1* ■ 2 ■ 3 ■ *1* ■ 2 ■ 3

💿 **5** In the next piece, the quavers marked * have a slur *and* a staccato dot. They should be joined smoothly to the previous note, but they should sound shorter than normal quavers.

TICK THE BOX WHEN YOU HAVE COMPLETED THIS SECTION ☐

💿 **6** The other new note length for Grade 3 is the **dotted quaver** (or dotted eighth note). For Grade 2 you learned that a dot after a note increases its length by half. A quaver is half of a crotchet, so a *dotted* quaver will be three-quarters of a crotchet: $\frac{1}{2} + \frac{1}{4} = \frac{3}{4}$.

A dotted quaver is normally followed by a semiquaver (♪.♬). Together these two notes take the space of one beat in $\frac{2}{4}$, $\frac{3}{4}$ or $\frac{4}{4}$ time. Listen to track 7, where you will hear the example played twice. The first time it is played very slowly, so that you can hear how the notes fit to a *semiquaver* pulse. The second time it is played up to speed.

💿 **7**

¼ ¼

This rhythm sounds jerky because a dotted quaver is three times longer than a semiquaver. Practise playing up and down the first five notes of the scale in all of the keys you have learned, using the dotted rhythms of piece 7. Remember to try this with your left hand as well as your right hand.

8 Now play the following piece. The first pair of quavers in each hand are normal quavers that should be played evenly, but the other quavers are all dotted. Listen to track 8 before you play the piece, and listen again afterwards to check that your rhythms were correct: a click track has been added to the music to help you get used to the dotted rhythms.

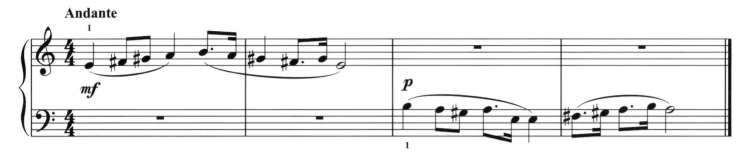

9 Here is another piece with dotted quavers. Like many pieces of sight-reading in Grade 3 it has two lines of music (eight bars in all). Some people fail to notice this in the exam, and stop at the end of the first line, thinking they have finished. Always look for the **double barline**, as this will tell you where the piece ends.

Try to read ahead of the beat that you are actually playing so that you don't need to hesitate when your eye has to leap to the second set of staves. Listen to track 9 before you play the piece, and listen again afterwards to check that your rhythms were correct. Take care over the timing in bar 4 where the right hand enters on the third beat of the bar.

TICK THE BOX WHEN YOU HAVE COMPLETED THIS SECTION ☐

⅜ TIME

10 There is a new time signature to learn for Grade 3. In ⅜ time, the upper figure tells you that there are three beats in a bar, just like ¾ time, but the lower figure tells you that in ⅜ you count in eighth notes, which are quavers.

The first piece at the top of the next page is written in ¾ and the second in ⅜ time. They sound similar, but look different because the notes in the second piece have been halved in length. Composers sometimes choose ⅜ to suggest a faster speed, for which you might count just one dotted crotchet beat in a bar, rather than three separate quaver beats. Listen to track 10 and see if you can hear this effect in the ⅜ version.

Now have a go at this piece for yourself. You don't have to play it as fast as the second version on the recording. It is more important to play the rhythms correctly, without any hesitations, than to risk the music sounding rushed.

TICK THE BOX WHEN YOU HAVE COMPLETED THIS SECTION ☐

TEMPO MARKINGS

 There are a few more foreign-language terms for tempo and mood that are useful to know for Grade 3. This list includes terms that were introduced in the two previous grades. You can hear how to pronounce these words by listening to track 11.

Andante	fairly slow
Andantino	slightly faster than *andante*
Moderato	moderate speed
Allegretto	fairly fast
Allegro	fast
Vivace	lively or quick
Alla marcia	in the style of a march
Cantabile	in a singing style
Espressivo	expressively
Giocoso	merrily
Grandioso	grandly
Grazioso	gracefully
Leggiero	lightly or delicately
Poco	a little (e.g. *poco allegro* – a little fast)
Scherzando	playfully or jokingly
Semplice	simply
Tempo di minuetto	at the speed of a minuet (steady 3 time)
Valse lente	slow waltz (slow 3 time)

The descriptive words in the second part of the list are sometimes combined with the tempo directions in the first part. For example, *Andante grazioso* means 'fairly slow and gracefully' while *Allegro leggiero* means 'fast and light'.

TICK THE BOX WHEN YOU HAVE COMPLETED THIS SECTION ☐

KEYS AND KEY SIGNATURES

 Grade 3 sight reading may be in any one of the following keys (those that are new at this grade are printed in **bold** type). The seventh note of the scale in minor keys normally has an accidental (shown by the black notes below) and the sixth note may also have an accidental (shown in brackets).

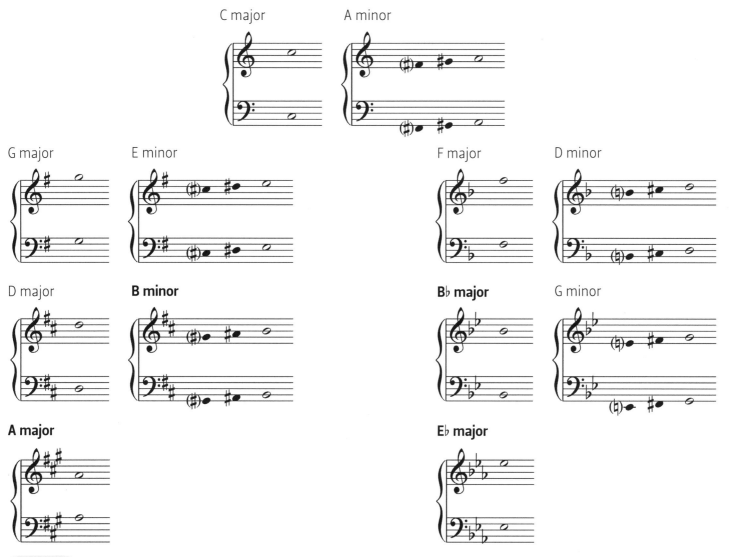

 Once you have learned C and F major, the name of every other key for Grade 3 sight reading can usually be worked out with three simple rules:

- If the key signature has sharps, and there are no accidentals in the music, the key is major and the name of the key is *one step above the last sharp in the key signature*. So, if the key signature ends with C♯ and there are no accidentals, the key is D major.

- If the key signature has flats, and there are no accidentals, the key is major and the name of the key is the same as the *next-to-last flat in the key signature*. So, if the next-to-last flat in the key signature is B♭ and there are no accidentals, the key is B♭ major.

- If there *are* accidentals, the key is minor and the name of the key is *one step above the name of the main accidental*. So, if you see the accidental C♯ in a piece where there is a B♭ in the key signature, the key is likely to be D minor.

The 'main accidental' in the last rule is the one on the seventh note of the scale – you will often see it just before the end of a piece. It is described as the 'main accidental' because, as mentioned above, the sixth note of a minor scale is also sometimes altered by an accidental.

If you have any doubt, the last left-hand note of the piece will usually help confirm the key. For example, if it is D, the key is probably either D major or D minor.

Now try some simple sight reading in the keys that are new for Grade 3. The first piece below has a key signature of two flats, and no accidentals. Because B♭ is the next-to-last flat in the key signature the music is in the key of **B♭ major**.

Before you start, get both hands into position by hovering your fingers over the notes needed, using the given fingering as a guide. The key signature tells you that black notes are needed for B♭ and E♭, and these notes are marked by arrows in this piece.

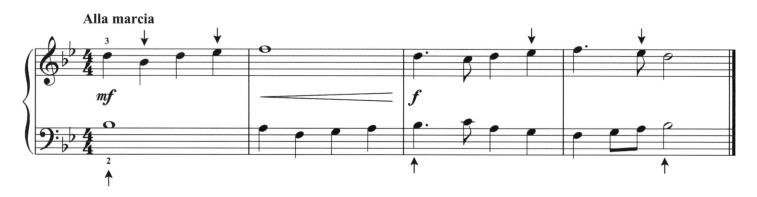

The next piece has a key signature of three flats, and no accidentals. E♭ is the next-to-last flat in the key signature, and so the key is **E♭ major**. Nearly half of the notes in this piece are black notes, as you can see from the arrows in the music, so concentrate hard on remembering that every B, E and A is a flat.

You may find it helps to play a scale of E♭ major (one of the scales you are learning for Grade 3) in both hands before you begin.

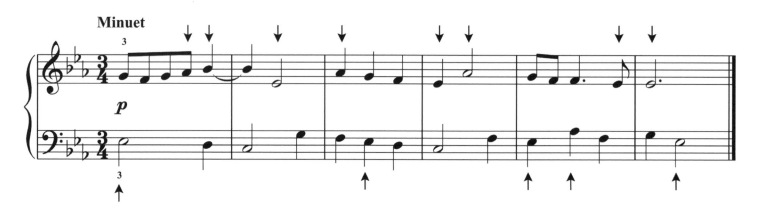

Piece 16 has a key signature of three sharps, and no accidentals. The name of the key is one step above the last sharp in the key signature. The last sharp is G♯ and so the name of the key is **A major**. Before you start, play a scale of A major in both hands to remind yourself of the black notes needed in this key. They are not marked by arrows this time, but there are 13 black notes to watch out for! Choose a fairly steady pulse to make sure you can manage all the semiquavers.

17 The last new key is **B minor**. It has a key signature of two sharps – F♯ and C♯, and you should expect to see an accidental for A♯ (and sometimes G♯ as well).

In the next piece you need to play A♮ in bar 3 in the right hand, but A♯ is needed in bar 1 and again just before the end of the piece. The seventh note of a minor scale will sometimes *not* have an accidental when it comes in the middle of the music, like A in bar 3 of this piece.

TICK THE BOX WHEN YOU HAVE COMPLETED THIS SECTION ☐

FINGERING

18 In sight reading for Grade 3 and higher, you may sometimes have to change from one five-finger position to another during the piece in order to reach more notes. This is called a **shift**, and at Grade 3 some extra fingering in the music will warn you of where this happens.

Look at the following music. It starts with the thumb on C, and then you are told to use the thumb again for G. You do this by swivelling your thumb underneath your third finger while playing E. This shifts your hand into a new position so that you can reach the high notes in the second half of the tune.

In sight-reading tests you will see just a single new fingering when a shift is needed, as shown above, but here is the same tune with every note fingered, so you can be sure of how to play it.

Practise this slowly until you are sure that there is no jolt or hesitation at the shift, and then gradually speed up.

It is not always necessary to shift position to reach a higher note. Another way is to use an **extension** which simply means moving your fingers a little further apart than normal. Again, this will often be indicated by some fingering in the music.

In the next tune you would normally use your fourth finger to play F in bar 2, but you would then run out of fingers before reaching A at the end of the bar. Instead, you are told to use your *third* finger to play F.

Practise using extensions by playing the previous tune for your right hand, and the next tune for your left hand.

 You may also see extra fingering given in sight-reading tests in places where it is not obvious how to finger the music. In the first two tunes below, the second finger of your right hand has to cross over your thumb, while in the third your left thumb has to pass under your second finger. Practise these exercises until you feel comfortable with the fingering.

Now try the following short pieces of sight reading, taking note of where the fingering changes. After you have played them, listen to the recordings.

 As soon as your right thumb plays C in the first bar, start moving your fifth finger down ready to play D in bar 2. Hold the C for its full length so there is no gap in the music as you shift position.

Moderato

This time the shift comes in your left hand. The fingering in bar 3 warns you to be ready for it.

You do not have to use the fingering printed in sight-reading tests, but it is well worth trying to do so, as it has been included to help you. It will help the music to flow as well as getting your fingers in position for the notes that follow. In the exam you will have 30 seconds to prepare the sight reading, and some of this time should be spent trying out any fingerings that look tricky.

TICK THE BOX WHEN YOU HAVE COMPLETED THIS SECTION

TWO NOTES TOGETHER IN THE SAME HAND

 In some Grade 3 sight reading tests there may be a few places where you will need to play two notes together in the same hand. If fingering is given for this, there will be two numbers. The upper number refers to the upper note, and the lower one to the lower note. So, in this example, your right hand should play F# with the third finger and D with the thumb.

Fingering won't be given if it is not necessary, as in the last bar above where you would use the same fingers as the start of the piece. In the following case, the left hand is already in position to use the fifth finger for F and the thumb for C in the last bar.

 The fingering should also be obvious in the next example, although you will need to extend your right thumb slightly downwards to reach the F♯ in the last bar.

 In the next example you are told to use your right thumb on A♭ at the start. You need to hold this note down, because it is a minim, while your fourth finger is playing D on the second beat of the bar. Your right thumb should then to drop to G while, at the same time, your fifth finger plays E♭.

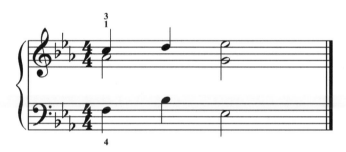

Practise the four short examples above until you feel confident in playing two notes together in the same hand. Then work through the following pieces of sight reading. Listen to the recording after you have played each one.

 Be ready for the right-hand shift at the end of bar 2 in this piece. In the last bar of the left-hand part, make sure your finger holds the F for three beats.

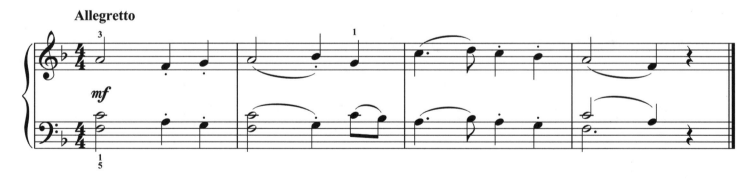

In this piece there is a shift for both hands at the end of bar 2: play smoothly, and watch out for the accidentals.

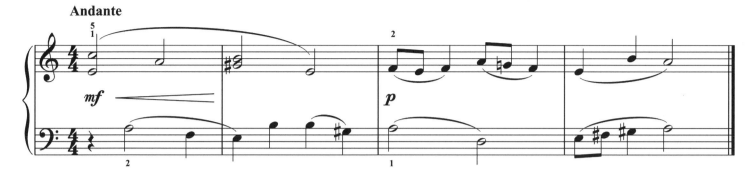

This is a reminder that some sight-reading tests contain *two* lines of music. Don't stop at the end of bar 4!

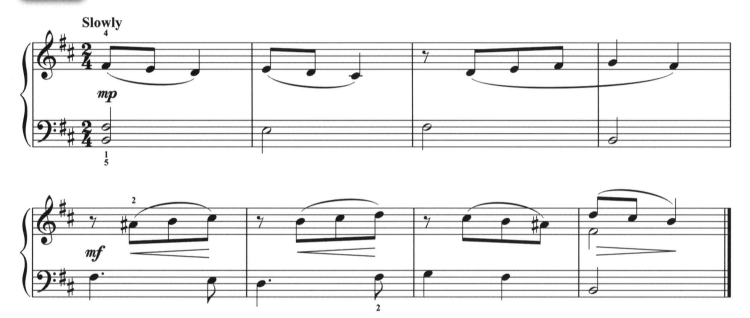

The fingering at the start of the next piece suggests that the fifth finger of your left hand should stay on C in every bar. In bar 3 the left hand has two notes (C and D) next to each other. These are written side-by-side for clarity, but you must still play them together. There is quite a clash of sounds on this beat. This is something that can make even good sight readers stop in their tracks if they haven't noticed it in advance – but the clash sounds fine if you play the music at a lively pace.

TICK THE BOX WHEN YOU HAVE COMPLETED THIS SECTION ☐

ON YOUR OWN

 Now you need plenty of practice in playing new pieces! The more you can do, the easier sight reading will become.

Work through the rest of this book, and use the recordings to check your playing. If you hear differences, try to work out why. Tick the box when you have played each piece, so that you keep trying new ones.

Things to check before starting a piece of sight reading:
- The time signature – are you going to count in twos, threes or fours?
- The tempo – how fast should you count? Remember to count yourself in for two whole bars.
- The key signature – are there any black notes to remember?
- Are there any accidentals, and do any of them affect later notes in the same bar?
- The fingering given for the start, and any changes of fingering during the piece.
- The dynamics – where should you play loudly and where softly?
- Any legato, staccato and accent markings.
- Are there any patterns in the music that will make it easier to read, and are there any leaps or rests that may be tricky?

Things to help you practise:
- Try playing slowly at first if that helps, and build up to a faster speed later:
  a regular pulse is more important than the speed at which you play.
- Try getting the notes and rhythm right first, and then play it again adding in changes of dynamics and details such as legato, staccato and accents.
- Try not to look at your fingers as you play, but keep your eyes fixed on the music.
  Get used to feeling your way around the keyboard without looking at it.
  Look ahead in the music to spot what is coming up.

Things to remember in the exam:
- The examiner will give you half a minute to look at the piece before asking you to play it.
  Use this time to try out the music – don't be afraid to do this, the examiner won't be listening!
  Play the opening and the ending, and perhaps any tricky bars.
- The examiner will tell you when to finish the try out and start playing for real.
- If you keep to a regular pulse at the marked speed and get most of the notes right,
  you will pass your sight reading!
- You will be heading for a top mark for sight reading if you also play fluently and bring out the expressive details in the music.
- Keep concentrating until you have given the last note its full length.
- **Try not to hesitate, even if you make a mistake.**
  Hesitations and stops are the most common reasons for a disappointing mark in sight reading.

Good luck with your Grade 3 sight reading!